A Let's-Read-and-Find-Out-Book™

Revised Edition

MY FIVE SENSES

by

ALIKI

A Harper Trophy Book

Harper & Row, Publishers

The *Let's-Read-and-Find-Out Book*™ series was originated by Dr. Franklyn M. Branley, Astronomer Emeritus and former Chairman of the American Museum-Hayden Planetarium, and was formerly co-edited by him and Dr. Roma Gans, Professor Emeritus of Childhood Education, Teachers College, Columbia University. Text and illustrations for each of the more than 100 books in the series are checked for accuracy by an expert in the relevant field. The titles available in paperback are listed below. Look for them at your local bookstore or library.

Air Is All Around You	Germs Make Me Sick!	Rockets and Satellites
Ant Cities	Get Ready for Robots!	The Skeleton Inside You
A Baby Starts to Grow	Glaciers	The Sky Is Full of Stars
The BASIC Book	Gravity Is a Mystery	Snakes Are Hunters
Bees and Beelines	Hear Your Heart	Snow Is Falling
The Beginning of the Earth	How a Seed Grows	Straight Hair, Curly Hair
Bits and Bytes	How Many Teeth?	The Sun: Our Nearest Star
Comets	How to Talk to Your Computer	Sunshine Makes the Seasons
Corn Is Maize	Hurricane Watch	Tornado Alert
Danger—Icebergs!	Is There Life in Outer Space?	A Tree Is a Plant
Digging Up Dinosaurs	Journey into a Black Hole	Turtle Talk
Dinosaur Bones	Look at Your Eyes	Volcanoes
Dinosaurs Are Different	Me and My Family Tree	Water for Dinosaurs and You
A Drop of Blood	Meet the Computer	What Happens to a Hamburger
Ducks Don't Get Wet	The Moon Seems to Change	What I Like About Toads
Eclipse	My Five Senses	What Makes Day and Night
Evolution	My Visit to the Dinosaurs	What the Moon Is Like
Fireflies in the Night	Oxygen Keeps You Alive	Why Frogs Are Wet
Flash, Crash, Rumble, and Roll	The Planets in Our Solar System	Wild and Woolly Mammoths
Fossils Tell of Long Ago	Rock Collecting	Your Skin and Mine

My Five Senses

Revised Edition

Published in hardcover by Thomas Y. Crowell, New York
First Harper Trophy edition, 1989.

Library of Congress Cataloging-in-Publication Data
Aliki.
  My five senses.

  (Let's-read-and-find-out science book)
  Summary: A simple presentation of the five senses, demonstrating some ways we use them.
  1. Senses and sensation—Juvenile literature.
[1. Senses and sensation] I. Title. II. Series.
QP434.A43 1989   612′.8   88-35350
ISBN 0-690-04792-4
ISBN 0-690-04794-0 (lib. bdg.)

  (Let's-read-and-find-out book)
  (A Harper Trophy book)
ISBN 0-06-445083-X

MY FIVE SENSES

for my sister, Helen Lambros

I can see! I see with my eyes.

I can hear! I hear with my ears.

I can smell! I smell with my nose.

I can taste! I taste with my tongue.

11

I can touch! I touch with my fingers.

I do all this with my senses.

I have five senses.

When I see the sun or a frog

or my baby sister,

I use my sense of sight. I am seeing.

When I hear a drum or a fire engine
or a bird,
I use my sense of hearing.
I am hearing.

When I smell soap or a pine tree
or cookies just out of the oven,
I use my sense of smell.
I am smelling.

When I drink my milk
and eat my food,
I use my sense of taste.
I am tasting.

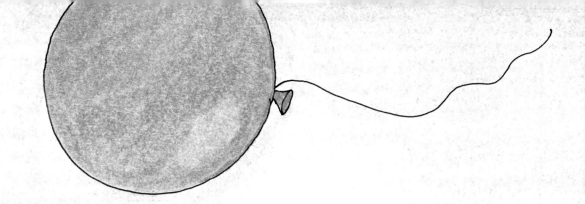

When I touch a kitten or a balloon or water,

I use my sense of touch.

I am touching.

Sometimes I use all my senses at once.

Sometimes I use only one.

I often play a game with myself.

I guess how many senses I am using at that time.

When I look at the moon and the stars,

I use one sense.

I am seeing.

When I laugh and play with my puppy,

I use four senses.

I see, hear, smell, and touch.

23

When I bounce a ball, I use three senses.
I see, hear, touch.

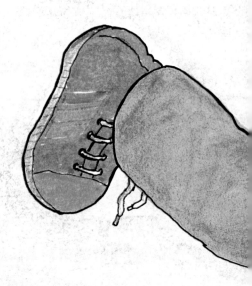

Sometimes I use more of one sense
and less of another.
But each sense is very important to me,
because it makes me aware.

To be aware is to see all there is to see...

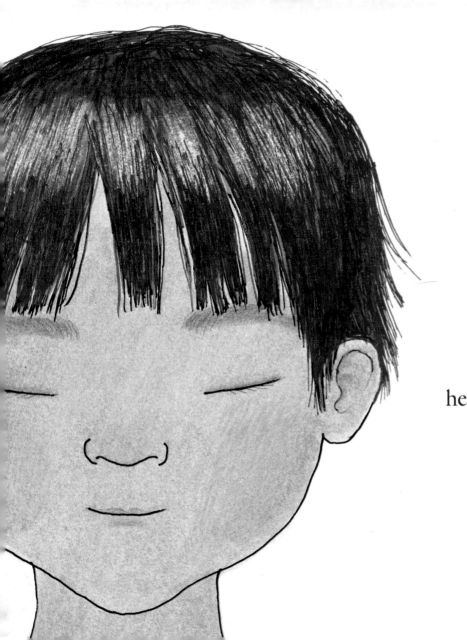

hear all there is to hear…

smell all there is to smell…

taste all there is to taste…

touch all there is to touch.

Wherever I go, whatever I do,
every minute of the day,
my senses are working.

They make me aware.